THE LAST MESSAGE RECEIVED

ALSO BY EMILY TRUNKO

DEAR MY BLANK:
SECRET LETTERS NEVER SENT

D BY
RUNKO
OPULAR TUMBLR

THE
LAST
MESSAGE
RECEIVED

ILLUSTRATED BY
ZOË INGRAM

CROWN NEW YORK

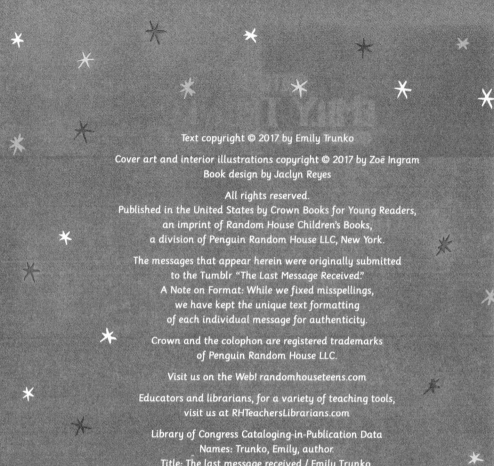

Published in the United States by Crown Books for Young Readers,
an imprint of Random House Children's Books,
a division of Penguin Random House LLC, New York.

The messages that appear herein were originally submitted
to the Tumblr "The Last Message Received."
A Note on Format: While we fixed misspellings,
we have kept the unique text formatting
of each individual message for authenticity.

Crown and the colophon are registered trademarks
of Penguin Random House LLC.

Visit us on the Web! randomhouseteens.com

Educators and librarians, for a variety of teaching tools,
visit us at RHTeachersLibrarians.com

Library of Congress Cataloging-in-Publication Data
Names: Trunko, Emily, author.
Title: The last message received / Emily Trunko.
Description: New York : Crown Books for Young Readers, 2017.
Identifiers: LCCN 2016021869 | ISBN 978-0-399-55776-7 (hardback) |
ISBN 978-0-399-55778-1 (epub)
Subjects: LCSH: Last words — Blogs — Juvenile literature. |
Farewells — Blogs — Juvenile literature. |
Tumblr (Electronic resource) — Juvenile literature.
Classification: LCC PN4393 .T78 2017 | DDC 808.86/051 — dc23

Printed in the United States of America

10 9 8 7 6 5 4 3 2 1

First Edition

THIS BOOK IS DEDICATED
TO ANYONE WHO'S EVER
RECEIVED A LAST MESSAGE.
MAY THESE LAST MESSAGES
HELP SHOW YOU THAT YOU'RE
NOT ALONE IN WHAT YOU'VE
GONE THROUGH.

INTROD

You never know which message you send or receive will be the last one you exchange with that person.

Unless you're one of the luckiest people in the world, you've probably had to deal with a friendship or relationship ending, or the death of someone you know. Some of your last conversations might have been commonplace, an everyday conversation before an untimely death, or an explosive fight between you and your ex best friend.

I came up with the idea for The Last Message Received Tumblr while I was sitting in my pajamas in my living room a few months before my sixteenth birthday. I sent out a call for submissions that very day and was amazed at the number that began pouring in. Since it began, The Last Message Received has affected many lives, including my own. It has helped bring closure to people who have had to deal with the sudden death of someone close to them, and it has shown suicidal people the shattering impact their actions would have on the people they would leave behind. It has taught so many

UCTION

people to be more careful with the messages they send, and to remind others how much they care about the people in their lives while they still have the chance to tell them how they feel.

After an interview I did with a local radio station, the man who was answering the phones shook my hand and thanked me. He said that my talking about The Last Message Received had inspired him to text his mother and tell her how much he loves her. That's the kind of impact I've been honored to see these powerful messages have on people. I think this Tumblr has made those who read its submissions much more aware and caring. In that gentle way, it has changed the world.

I hope the messages in these pages, which show human emotions ranging from heartbreak to love to joy to sorrow and anything in between, can change your lives in the way they've changed the lives of many of the Tumblr's followers.

EMILY TRUNKO
January 2017

 YOU

were always my

 SKY,

but i was just another

 STAR

in yours.

YOU HAVE SO MANY
PERSONALITIES

AND I DON'T

LIKE ANY

OF THEM

The last message I received from my best friend since first grade. I'm bipolar and he decided he couldn't deal with the troubles that came with being around me.

I never would have slept with you if I knew 1% of what I know about you now. Just please go away forever. I want to pretend you and the baby don't exist. Please respect that. That's my truth. No response needed.

This was not the first time he said this to me, but I made sure it was the last time. We loved each other so much we imploded. He broke my heart and nearly destroyed me. We were not and are not good for each other. He's unstable and beyond anything I could've done for him. While it's probably best and safest he's not in our lives, it kills me that my son has no father. He is missing everything. My son is amazing.

DON'T WORRY yourself
TOO MUCH ABOUT ME.
I'LL BE FINE.
I HAVE TO RUN, babe.
ONLY 9 MORE DAYS!

He said this two days before his convoy exploded in Libya and a week before I held his hand and felt his heart stop beating. It's been two years since and I still wake up sometimes thinking that if I call he'll answer the phone.

I miss my friend.

I'm sorry. But I have no desire to pursue that. It wouldn't be fair to pretend that I do. I hold nothing against you but I just have no wish to rebuild something that turned into a mistake for us both.

If that is what you want. I don't agree but I'm willing to let you have your way. It probably wouldn't work anyway. I have changed a lot.

One of my best friends in life. We got kind of romantically involved for like a week. About a month later, he suddenly stopped talking to me. Six months after, I initiated contact saying I wanted to be friends again. He said that he couldn't be friends with someone he had been involved with. And now we are back to being strangers. I never saw our friendship as a mistake. And it hurts that it meant so little to him.

JUST
REMEMBER
YOU'RE THE ONE
WHO RUINED
IT.

After I dumped him because he punched me in the stomach

Are you still up?

Hi, where'd you go?

My long-distance boyfriend and I talked on the phone every night before we went to sleep. We were in the middle of our nightly phone call when a friend stopped by his place. He asked if he could call me back in a few minutes. I fell asleep while waiting for him to call me. His final phone call and text at 12:40 a.m. was the last message I received from him. He died of a seizure in the middle of the night. I never said goodbye or "I love you" for the final time. I still feel such guilt, anger, and sadness about this, even after all these years.

i'm not going to drive drunk. i promise.
i'll talk to you later, love.

He did. He was killed later that night in a head-on
collision with another drunk driver. He was 22.

I'M SORRY
IF I HURT
YOU.
I JUST LOVE
HER,
I ALWAYS DID.

After falling hard for a boy who told me he'd never
leave. We haven't spoken since. I miss him so much.

hey, I had fun last night!

Yeah . . . please don't contact me.

why? did I do something wrong?

I was just thinking about it and idk I just don't really like you.

oh okay.

I just can't be seen with someone that looks like you do.

No offense lol.

My father's last words to me before he threw me down the stairs. He had been beating me for years, and my mother never knew. (He always did it when she was at work, and I didn't think that she would believe me.) He was diagnosed bipolar but refused to take his meds and was having a particularly bad day. He was screaming at my mom about something, and I ran down the stairs because I was scared he was going to hit her. Because I intervened, he lost his temper and backhanded me and kicked me in front of my mom. That was the last straw. She packed our things and said she was leaving him. (They weren't happy anymore, but were staying together to co-parent.) I cleaned out my room and was trying to run down the stairs, but he grabbed me and threw me down instead.

He has a new family now. And I pray he's not beating his new kids.

You are the world's most WRETCHED child, and the BIGGEST mistake I ever made. Congratulations on finally RUINING our family.

YOU NEED TO BE REALISTIC.

My best friend after I told him I was approached by a publisher for my novel. I never replied and haven't heard from him since. The book will be out in January.

Hey, are you still coming to my graduation banquet?

Nah, I'll pass

Ok. So I take it as our friendship is over?

Yes

One word that ended it all. It started out with a small fight, but it went downhill from there and we just grew apart. We tried to work it out, but I felt like she didn't make an effort to save this friendship. A few weeks after we stopped talking she sent me this text and I chose my ego over this friendship.

I JUST DIDN'T HAVE THAT **excitement** ABOUT SEEING YOU.

You never came.

Why?

Because I don't love you anymore.

I invited him to come watch my play every day for a month, and he always said he was gonna come because that's what friends do, but then he didn't show up. I asked him why and this is what I got.

PLEASE STOP
USING MY
NETFLIX.

SeRiOUSLY
STOP.

I broke up with him over Facebook after we dated
for five years. Shittiest thing I've ever done.

I think we should break up.

Don't say that butt head.

I'm not joking I swear . . . I've just been thinking and idk I just don't see you in my future. you're amazing and we've always been really great friends I always have awesome times with you and it's nothing personal. It's just I can't picture myself having a future with you in it.

If that's how you feel.

I'm sorry, I wish it was different I just can't see it.

This is the last time I let myself fall for you then. I think it's better if we don't speak from now on.

She couldn't see a life with me. I'm having a hard time seeing one without her.

I'm drunk but

I really do love you

He never made it home that night. A drunk driver ran straight
into him doing 50 mph on a 30-mph road. He was my best friend.

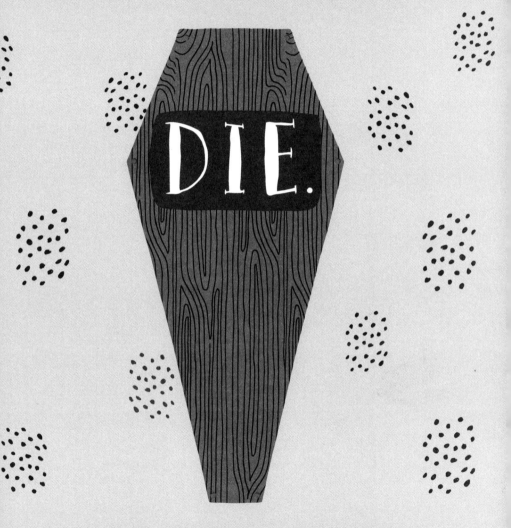

I WISH YOU WOULD DIE.

We dated for almost a year, and I am currently four months pregnant with his child. We broke up and he's mad I didn't get an abortion.

We are now both single.

You're being serious?

Yeah.

So you're breaking up with me?

Yes.

Right, okay then.

So that's it?

Yep.

I wanted to think it was a joke. But it wasn't. It's been six months and I still love him. I think that's one of the worst ways to break up with someone.

you should've
been my clear choice
and I'm such a
<u>DUMBASS</u>
for not seeing that.

I was reading our old messages and I just missed us so much.

he told me he loved me. made me feel like i was his everything. six weeks later he accused me of cheating on him with my gay best friend. then broke up with me. a month later he sent me this.

I REALLY LOVE YOU.

YOU KNOW THAT, RIGHT?

She went swimming in the sea. They never found her body. They think it was suicide. She was my girlfriend of two years. I really loved her too.

Goodnight, MY love, and SWeet DReAMS.

My crush said this the day before he got deployed for army duties. He got shot in the chest and died instantly.

I'm ready to be friends again!

I don't care.

We haven't spoken since.

I love you, never forget that.

I loved you.

She moved on. I didn't.

FRANKLY, I
WASN'T
READY.

I have to be honest...

You just broke my heart

Not my intention

I know this

Sorry

I

thought

you

were

a

better

person

than

this.

The boy who looked at me like I was the stars.
I'll never forgive myself for breaking my best
friend's heart. He hasn't spoke to me in 11 months.

> Go towards the bathroom.
> There is space.

> Are you still here?

I was trying to meet up with my friend at a concert but I was having trouble because it was crowded and loud. I was about to leave but then I saw her coming through the crowd like the beautiful little ray of light that she was. We danced together for one song before I decided I needed to leave because it was getting late. She told me she loved me and gave me a hug. The next morning when I came into work she hadn't showed up for her shift yet. I called and sent her texts, asking if she overslept. We found out a couple of hours later that she had swerved off the road and hit a tree on her way to work that morning, and she was gone. She was only a couple weeks away from graduating high school. Every time I think of her, I just think of how happy and blissful she looked the night before, and I know she's resting easy, but it still breaks my heart every day.

Nadiaaaa

I love you, Nads

Nadia texted me her name to let me know of her new phone number—her newest phone number, as she had to change her number frequently to avoid her abusive ex-boyfriend. On November 28, he shot her in the back of her head. She died the next day. It was her birthday.

i'm coming up to the roundabout now, i'll be there in 10 minutes.

He was on his way to pick me up when a car
sideswiped him and his car rolled down a hill.
He didn't wake up. They didn't catch the driver.

Break a leg today. ;-)

Be better if you were there.

I fell out with my dad after he did something that hurt me when I found out, which he later tried to explain away as "people carrying stories," so I told him I wouldn't be at his upcoming wedding. On the day of the wedding I sent a good luck text anyway, which he replied to, and I ignored it. We didn't communicate after that, mostly due to being very alike and stubborn, and six months later I was at his bedside as he passed away from a brain hemorrhage.

I don't regret not going to the wedding. I desperately regret not getting in touch with him, and will until I die.

It's not that I don't love you anymore, it's just that I never did.

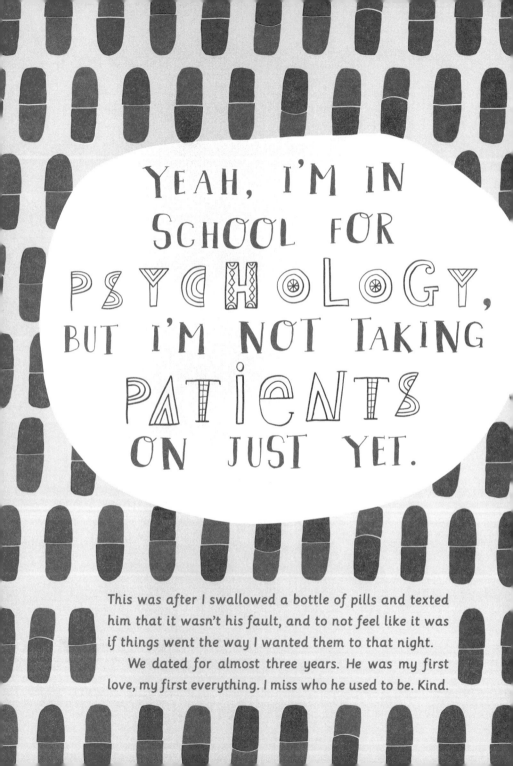

YEAH, I'M IN SCHOOL FOR PSYCHOLOGY, BUT I'M NOT TAKING PATIENTS ON JUST YET.

This was after I swallowed a bottle of pills and texted him that it wasn't his fault, and to not feel like it was if things went the way I wanted them to that night.

We dated for almost three years. He was my first love, my first everything. I miss who he used to be. Kind.

Your phone call woke me up.

I miss you so much . . .

I moved on and you should too.

I stopped trying after this, but I miss him every day.

I told you to leave me alone.

I love you.

We sent those two texts at the exact same time. I, the first message, and he, the latter. Neither of us replied.

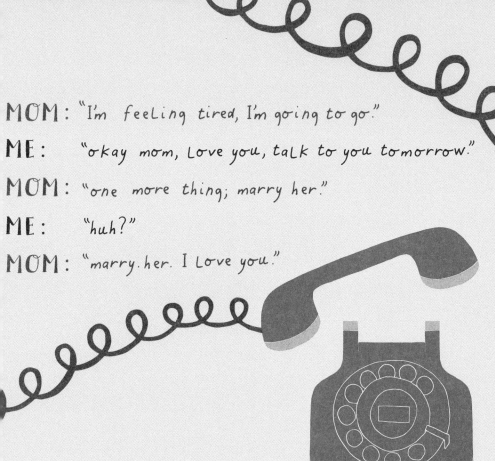

MOM: "I'm feeling tired, I'm going to go."

ME: "okay mom, Love you, talk to you tomorrow."

MOM: "one more thing; marry her."

ME: "huh?"

MOM: "marry. her. I Love you."

This was the last conversation I had with my mom before she died from complications from an accident she was in a few weeks before. She had only met my girlfriend twice before she passed, but she knew we were meant to be. My mom died in January 2011; I proposed in December that year. We have since gotten married and have a daughter. Not a day goes by without me wishing my mom was around to see her granddaughter. My mom knew. She just . . . knew.

MY BABY,

REMEMBER THAT NO MATTER
WHAT I WILL ALWAYS BE INSIDE
YOUR HEART SPREADING MY
LOVE THROUGHOUT YOUR LIFE.

I KNOW YOU'VE BEEN HAVING A
HARD TIME BUT JUST REMEMBER
THAT IF YOU CLOSE YOUR EYES,
I'LL BE THERE ALWAYS.

I'M SORRY I CAN'T BE WITH YOU
ANYMORE BUT I CAN'T LIVE WITH
MYSELF ANYMORE.

I WILL ALWAYS LOVE YOU AND
YOUR FATHER BUT I NEED TO BE IN
MY PLACE OF PEACE RIGHT NOW.

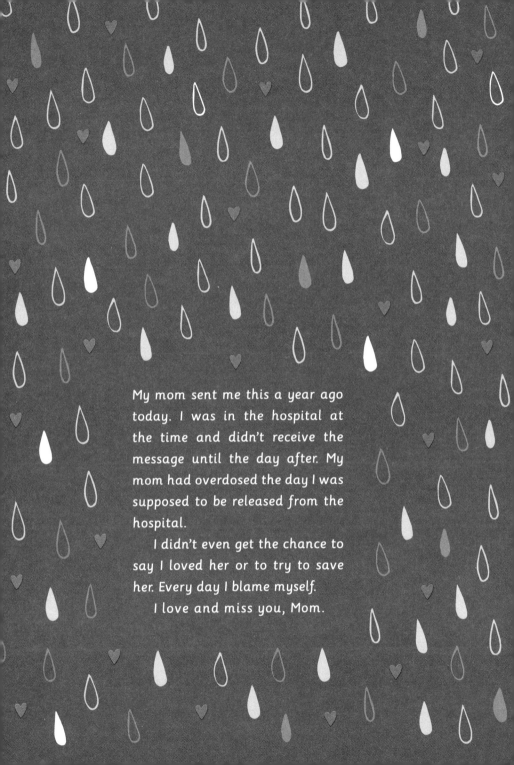

My mom sent me this a year ago today. I was in the hospital at the time and didn't receive the message until the day after. My mom had overdosed the day I was supposed to be released from the hospital.

I didn't even get the chance to say I loved her or to try to save her. Every day I blame myself.

I love and miss you, Mom.

I didn't grab you and kiss you for the sake of it. That's how I felt. That's how I always felt. That's the only way I could say it because I just couldn't find the words.

Don't hold back in life. You can have anything you want, you're young and beautiful... I wish I tried harder for us.

My (ex) girlfriend of one year and seven days sent this to me a year after our breakup and on the day it would have been our two-year anniversary.

damn. I love you.
I love you so much.

He broke up with me because I'm not his religion and he thinks God hates him for the fact that he was in a relationship with me.

Say your good by, see u
never—On my way! Gone

What??

By the time I replied, she was already dead. My best
friend sent this message and then hung herself.

I HAVE IT UNDER CONTROL, I PROMISE :)

He died the next day of an esophageal tear because he, as a male, was too embarrassed to ask for help with his bulimia. He is the only reason I decided to recover from my own eating disorder.

I HOPE THE UNIVERSE PAYS YOU IN DOUBLE EVERYTHING YOU'RE DOING TO ME.

Said my two-year girlfriend to me when I left her because I couldn't stand that toxic relationship anymore. After that she sent me a Facebook message saying she wished I was dead. I never answered. We haven't spoken for almost two years now.

I know that

I was a really good friend to you. And I was a cool gf ok.

I just want you to know

I would die for you. But I won't live for you. Please don't text me again except about the stuff you're going to return. It hurts too much.

Sweet!! I found all the Foo Fighters discs you made for me!!

Woohoo

My best friend, Eryn. Our "friendship" was not easily described because we were also lovers from time to time.

Eryn was hit by a train four hours after this text conversation. I still write her and listen to the Foo Fighters when I'm sad.

I'm so sorry. Don't follow me.

This was from a boy I had been dating for almost
two years. I was head over heels in love with him.
He killed himself that night. I'm still not over it.

I'M GONNA LOOK MY BEST WHEN I GO TO HEAVEN.

He sent me this right before he shot himself. It had a picture of him smiling, wearing his new suit. We had broken up exactly a month before.

Btw

Your soul inspired my outfit today

He sent a picture of his outfit, too. All black.

IT'S eaSieR to

YOU
than to
miss YOU.

DON'T KILL YOURSELF CAUSE THEN PEOPLE WILL BLAME ME FOR IT.

Said my ex-boyfriend when we were breaking up. All in one night I found out he lied to me about being with other people, that his feelings changed and he no longer would ever love me. He told me not to kill myself because people would blame him. Not because he didn't want me to die. Because he didn't want to be held responsible for my depressive state if I went over the edge. We were together for two years. I moved 3,000 miles away from family and friends to be with him. I just got sick after a bad car crash and grew extremely depressed and fell into bipolar disorder. These were the results of that in my love life.

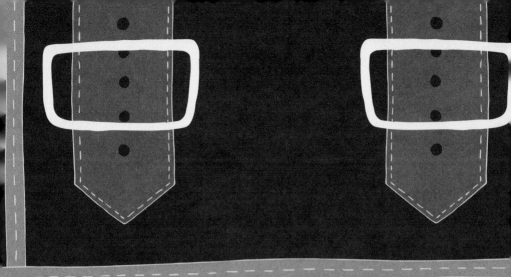

SUITCASES ARE REPLACEABLE, JUST LIKE YOU.

My boyfriend of a year (after borrowing his suitcase and not returning it)

It's like you bombed into my life, and I'm still here picking up the pieces from every argument, every teary eyed phone call, and I just ache all over but you fix it.

You're like antibiotics.

A little bit of you makes me feel so much better, but if I get too much I become addicted and I'm terrified of not being able to cope with it.

Together on and off for years, the distance got too much. Such a beautiful disaster.

I want to go back to the first night I met you and restart everything. I want to treat you right and make up for everything I did wrong . . . that's if you let me, though?

I didn't. He had too many chances. I still saved this text from him, though . . . almost four years later.

THE NEXT TIME YOU TRY TO
COMMIT SUICIDE
I HOPE YOU SUCCEED,
THEN I HAVE A LEGIT REASON
NOT TO LOOK AT YOUR
DUMB FACE
ANY MORE.

He was my boyfriend for six years and dumped me because I got diagnosed with severe depression. This was his last text after I woke up at the ICU, 24 hours after he left me.

YOU ARE A BLACK HOLE; YOU DRAINED ME.

miss u like crazy glue lol

A very good friend and the guy who was my first kiss sent me this message a week before he was murdered. He was 24. Every year on his birthday, I write this on a note and send it up in a balloon.

do you have any advice for me?

i have a really bad feelin

The last message I received from my friend the day she was killed by a suicide bomber in Iraq. I had just left the same post five days earlier. I replied, but she never got the message. I told her never to stand out in the open. She was killed while standing out in the open. It haunts me to this day.

I wish you had looked at me like you did at sunsets and the stars.

A month or so after our breakup, my ex-boyfriend got stoned and sent me this. He never knew it, but I did look at him like I did the stars and sunsets. He just never noticed. He never knew it. He still doesn't.

SO MAYBE IT WAS IN THE CARDS. WE JUST GOT DEALT THE WRONG HAND.

The truest words I've ever known, and that's what hurt the most.

Please don't cry. We both knew it would happen. Everything we had was amazing and I will never forget you.

We broke up this Saturday because I'm leaving for Brazil for good real soon. That's the message he sent me when he saw me walking away from his apartment for the very last time. We dated for seven months.

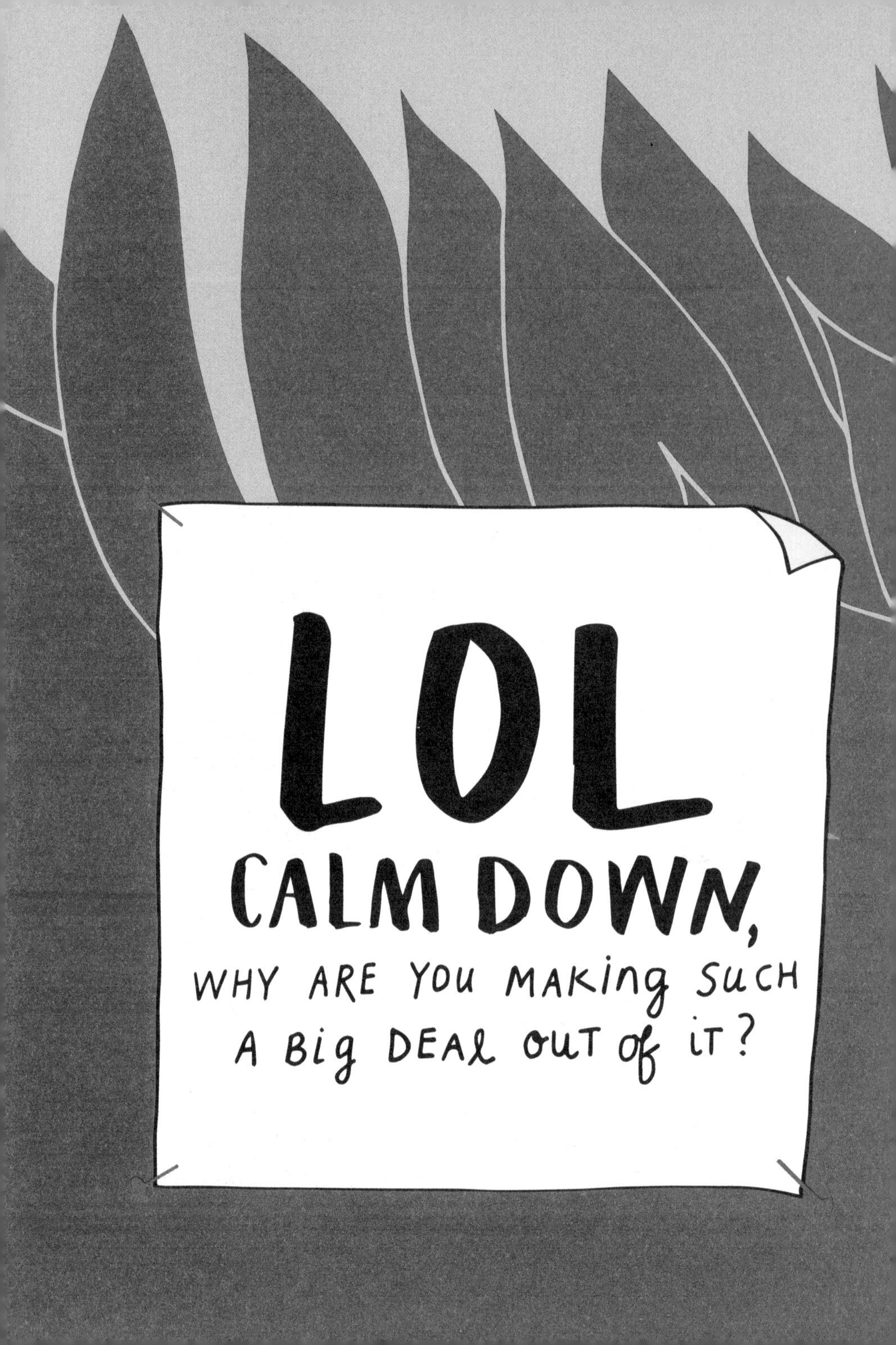
LOL
CALM DOWN,
WHY ARE YOU MAKING SUCH
A BIG DEAL OUT OF IT?

What he said after the third time he sexually assaulted me. The first was when we were at a movie theater with friends. He shoved his hand up my skirt. I was 12 and too scared to say anything. The second was at a friend's house. I got there and realized so was he, so I left the room to call my parents and tell them to pick me up. He followed me, pinned me down on the floor, ripped off my clothes, and assaulted me for what seemed like hours. I got home and received a message from him saying that he had gotten to the friend's house before I did and set up cameras, so if I told a soul, he would send the photos to everyone. I was 13. The last time was at a middle school reunion, and somehow I ended up on the subway with him and he apologized for what had happened years ago. Then minutes later, he grabbed me and held me down on the seats. We got to our stop and I ran, but not before he grabbed my arm, pulled me back, and was about to pull my clothes off. He let me go when I elbowed him in the stomach. I was 17. I went home and messaged him: "If you ever touch me again, I don't care what you have on me, I will collect all my friends and we will find you. I will personally rip your dick off."

You're so beautiful

I'm drinking

Am I just beautiful because you're drunk?

He never called me beautiful when he was sober.

I'M *choosing*
MY NEW *life*
OVER YOU.

The last message he sent me. We were 488 miles apart.

Let's just break for the next week or so, and see where we are at.

Unless you want something else.

No that's fine, gives me some hope hah!

If you need longer though, that can be decided after the week.

I love him more than I've ever loved anyone.

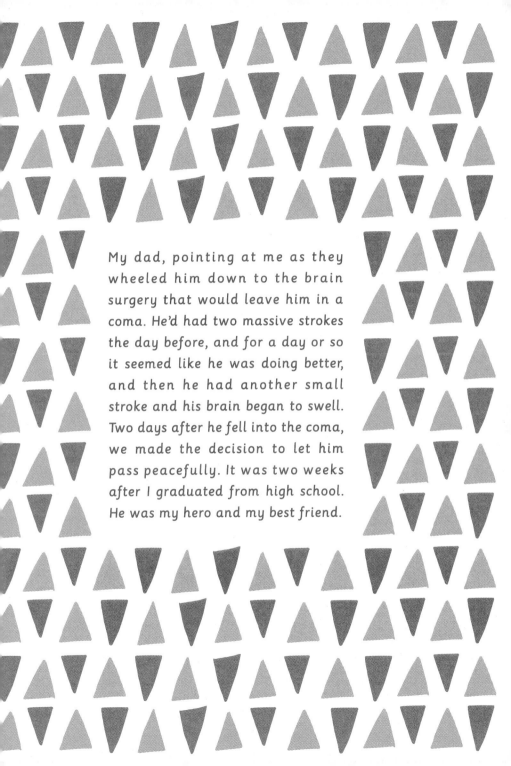

My dad, pointing at me as they wheeled him down to the brain surgery that would leave him in a coma. He'd had two massive strokes the day before, and for a day or so it seemed like he was doing better, and then he had another small stroke and his brain began to swell. Two days after he fell into the coma, we made the decision to let him pass peacefully. It was two weeks after I graduated from high school. He was my hero and my best friend.

I'M SORRY

I PUT SUCH

SHAME

ON THE FAMILY

NAME.

My uncle, in the fourth letter he sent me from jail

YOUR PRIORITIES ARE
OUT of ORDER
BUT YOU KNOW WHAT?
I'M DONE TALKING TO YOU.
I DON'T WANT TO HEAR FROM YOU AGAIN.
I'M DONE DEALING WITH YOU GOOD LUCK WITH YOUR LIFE.
—DAD

My dad and I had gotten into a fight. I told him
I couldn't call him because I was studying for finals.
This was his response. We haven't talked since.

This was the last photo taken of my dog Roxy. We had to put her down because her cancer progressed too far. I received this picture on my phone, sent from my parents. They asked if I wanted to FaceTime to say something to her, or to just say goodbye. I said no, because of how much it hurt to know the dog I grew up with wouldn't be there to greet me when I came back from school out of state. I will forever wish I had said yes.

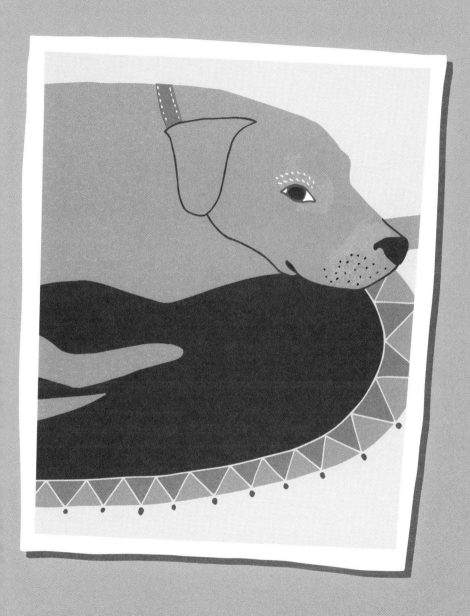

Pls dont kiss anyone else

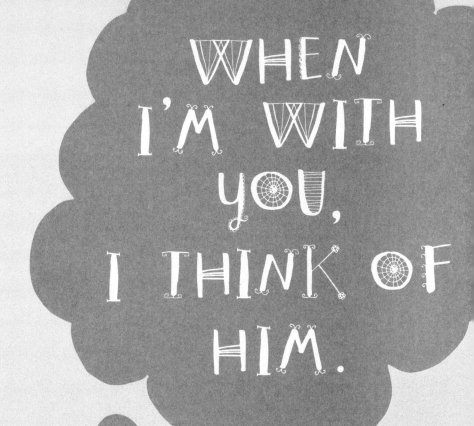

"Why did you come back and kiss me?"
"BECAUSE I WANTED YOU TO MAKE ME HAPPY."
"but it seems like I don't make you happy anymo
"NO. YOU DON'T. SORRY."

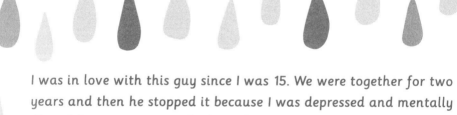

I was in love with this guy since I was 15. We were together for two years and then he stopped it because I was depressed and mentally ill and he was too scared of it. After two years he came back, we kissed and he told me that he never stopped loving me. I was so happy. A couple of days later, he broke up with me with these words. I went over to his home to speak with him and to give him a book that we liked to read, where I wrote that I was sure that he was my twin soul and that I loved him. He read it, threw it to me, and left.

PLEASE DON'T CALL, I CAN'T HEAR YOUR VOICE. THIS IS FOR THE BEST AND EVERYTHING WILL BE OKAY. I LOVE YOU, BABY, AND I WILL MISS YOU, SO DAMN MUCH. STAY SAFE AND KICK ASS IN AUSTIN.

We are both closet lesbians and had a short but passionate five-month relationship. We knew our families would not approve and I had to move nine hours away for college very soon. I was willing to change my plans and go to a local college instead because I wanted to stay with her. She didn't let me. She texted me this shortly after we kissed goodbye.

I DON'T SEE a future WITH you.

I was in a near-fatal car accident. My boyfriend that I had been dating for two years started to pull away, and this was the last thing he said to me after finding out that, due to head trauma, I had developed epilepsy. Those words play in my head every time I tell someone I have epilepsy now.

flipping awesome!

making money, doing school, sober a year in june.

life don't get much better.

that's so goooood!

really happy to hear.

Last message with an old friend who I had lost touch with because of his spiraling drug problem. I spoke to him about three weeks before he overdosed, and he had never sounded so happy to be sober.

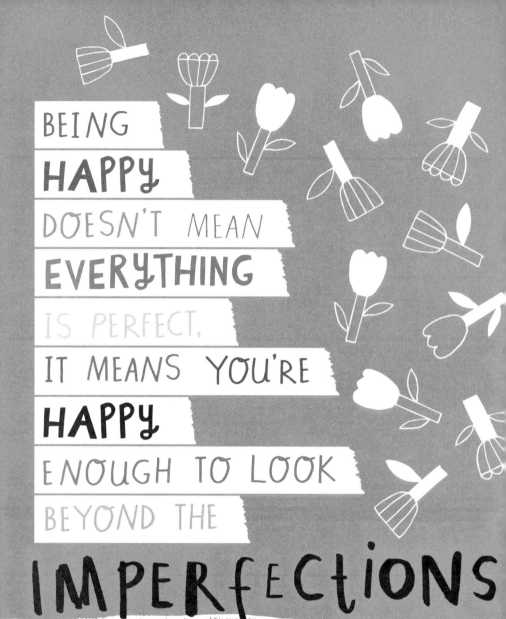

BEING **HAPPY** DOESN'T MEAN **EVERYTHING** IS PERFECT, IT MEANS YOU'RE **HAPPY** ENOUGH TO LOOK BEYOND THE **IMPERFECTIONS**

My friend posted this on Facebook a few days before she overdosed on heroin. She was 21. Life's not fair, but her memory keeps me alive.

YOU'RE AN ATTENTION-SEEKING SLUT!

DON'T CALL ME AGAIN.

He cheated on me more times than I can count on my fingers and toes. When I confronted him it was the last time we ever spoke.

JUST PUT a BANDAID on IT,

I'LL KISS IT BETTER WHEN I NEXT SEE YOU.

My ex when I messaged him that I was bleeding from the glass he threw at me after an argument. I left right then.

YES, A BABY IS A MIRACLE,

BUT NOT IN OUR LIFE.

The last message he sent me after I told him
I'm pregnant and I want to keep the baby.

I NEVER WANTED YOU anyway.
I TRIED TO COMMIT SUICIDE
3 TIMES WHILE I WAS pregnan
WITH YOU.

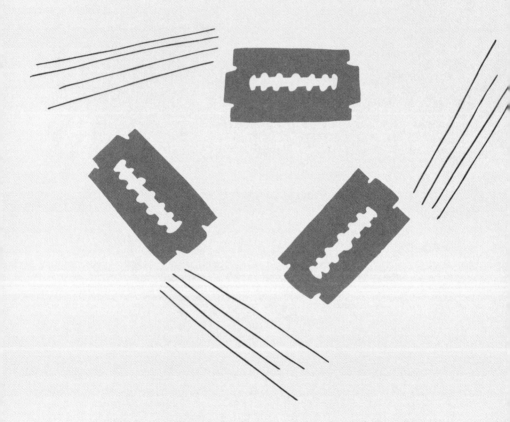

My mum, as she was leaving for the last time. It's been
nearly nine years. I was 16. I don't want you either.

THANK YOU FOR THE VISIT iCed BUns SO MUCH NICER WHEN eaTen IN COMPANY.

The last text I got from my gramps before he passed away.

YOU MAKE ME FEEL YOUNGER EVERY TIME YOU KISS MY CHEEK, DARLING.

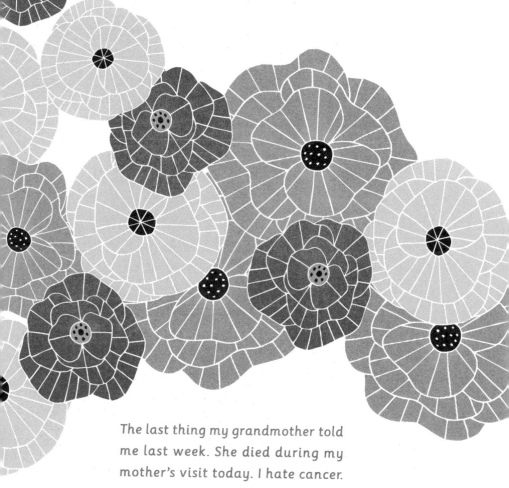

The last thing my grandmother told me last week. She died during my mother's visit today. I hate cancer.

WE WERE TWO TREES
WHO GREW TOGETHER.

WE JUST ENDED UP
GROWING IN
DIFFERENT DIRECTIONS.

I love you

But I'm not in love with you

My first relationship was a cliché, so it
seems fitting that it ended with one.

TALK TO YOU LATER. LOVE YOU BIG BROTHER

The way my sister usually ended a voice mail. I found her dead today. When our brother died in 2012, she started a downward spiral, and I sadly ignored it. I am comforted knowing that they are together again.

I'M REALLY SORRY.
I DIDN'T REALIZE HOW MUCH
IT WAS HURTING YOU ALL SO MUCH.
I THINK I'VE ALWAYS HAD IT TOO EASY.
I'M REALLY TRYING. I...

SORRY, I WAS REALLY BUSY THIS WEEKEND
DID YOU STILL NEED TO TALK?

SPENCE? CALL, PLEASE.

SPENCE.

My brother hung himself that day. After his last text he called me and left a voice mail. I didn't call him back right away because hanging out with my friends was more important and I didn't want to listen to him complain anymore. When I called him back, it was too late.

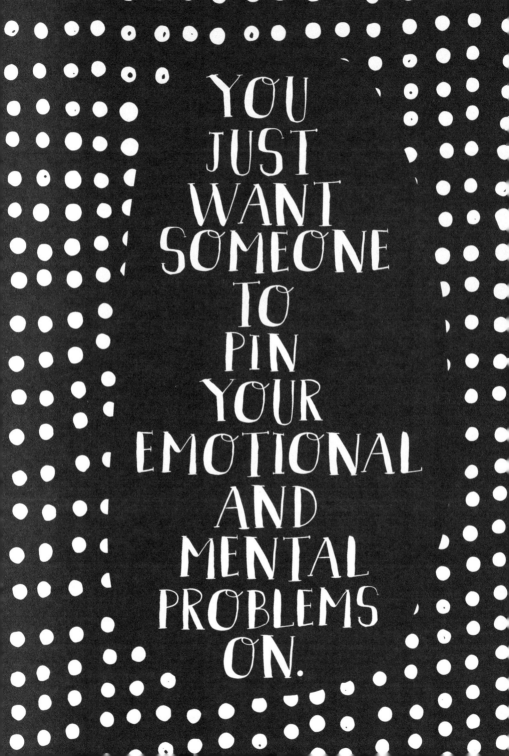

YOU JUST WANT SOMEONE TO PIN YOUR EMOTIONAL AND MENTAL PROBLEMS ON.

I'M **SORRY.**
I WANT TO GIVE
YOU
ALL OF ME,
BUT
I feel like I'D BE
GIVING YOU SOMETHING

BROKEN.

I began having anxiety attacks because I was falling in love with him, but he wouldn't let himself receive my love. He believed he wasn't good enough for me, and also wasn't ready for the deep intimacy we were starting to build. I had to be the strong one and end our relationship before we grew bitter towards each other for not getting what we wanted/needed from the other. He said this to me before he walked away the last night we saw each other. I still miss him every minute.

Delete my number too thanks

Fine

Delete mine too

I did

I'll never call you

Even if I'm dying

Okay then

A text from my girlfriend of two years, apologizing for not being able to join my family and me for my 21st-birthday dinner. When I got back to my apartment, I called her, and she told me she'd met someone else. She broke up with me on my birthday. Most people have great stories on their 21st. Mine sucked. Really bad.

You are such a beautiful
person and I hope you find

SOMEONE

who can give you everything
you deserve. I will

HATE

them for being able to
be someone I couldn't be for you,
but I just want to see you

HAPPY.

I wish it could have been

DIFFERENT.

I wanted it to be him so badly.

you're the only girl who matters to me

I wasn't.

30 SECONDS

I WOULD LOVE 30 SECONDS TO GIVE YOU A HUG TO LOOK IN YOUR EYES AND SEE YOU SMILE TO HEAR THE SOUND OF YOUR VOICE IN PERSON TO DRINK IN THE SCENT THAT MOVES AROUND YOU TO SEE YOU HAPPY. HAVE A GOOD WEEKEND. *HUGS* —ME

Received the email before he went on a weekend trip. The next day, he flipped the vehicle he was driving. He died two nights later. It will be a decade this year, but I still think of him often.

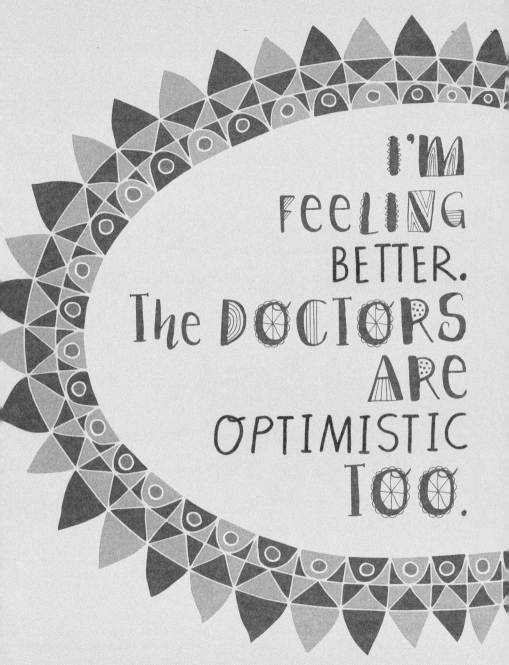

I'M FEELING BETTER. The DOCTORS ARE OPTIMISTIC TOO.

My friend of seven years a week before she died of brain cancer.

The last text I got from him. I was diagnosed with a heart condition; we had been on and off for over a year. When he found out I needed heart surgery, he left because he thought I might die in the operating room. My surgery is in three weeks.

:(I miss talking to my baby girl. I miss your presence and you so much

Blah this day's been so hard and depressing for me. I can't think straight without you blahhh

I didn't reply that day because I was mad at him, and that same night he had sex with someone else.

ASK THE WIZARD FOR A HEART.

I'd met the most amazing man—we planned to grow old together and we just knew we were right for each other. But we both suffered badly from depression and had huge fears too. He had texted me and asked me to go pick him up from the city and I'd said no. His last text to me (or anyone) was to ask the wizard for a heart (implying that I was heartless like the Tin Man). It really hurt and I felt awful. I didn't reply. We never spoke again. One day later he committed suicide.

I live with it every day. I miss him every day more than anything in the world.

I'm so disappointed in you

Don't try to contact me anymore . . . I have nothing more to say to you . . . you have none of my support

Good to know. Thanks, Dad. Bye.

The last thing my dad ever said to me after finding out I was pregnant at 17.

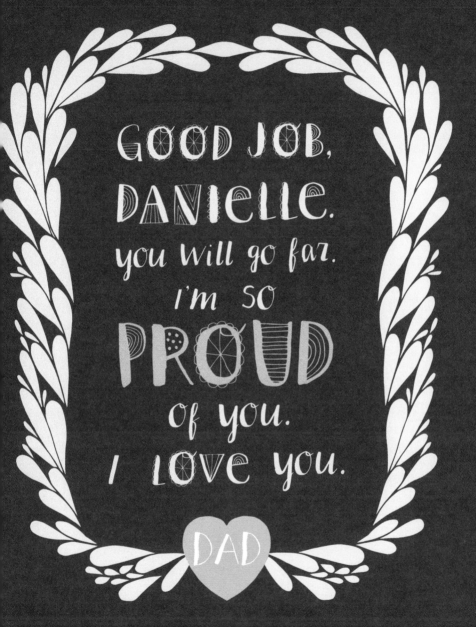

GOOD JOB,
DANIELLE.
you will go far.
I'm SO
PROUD
of you.
I LOVE you.

DAD

This was the last thing my father ever
wrote me before he died two years ago.

This was the last sentence my mother ever said to me. I was 15, going to my first homecoming at a new school in a new town. She was in a nursing home recovering from hip surgery because her cancer had eaten through her bones. It was the last thing she ever said at all. I didn't want to go to the dance, because I wanted to be with her every moment, but she insisted. She passed away the next day.

It's been six years and I still hate when people say that sentence to me.

I'm clean now, it's so liberating. I wish your mom would do the same, you kids deserve it. Love you -Uncle

Really?! Thats wonderful!! I'm so happy for you and the girls! I'm glad you're home now too.

I hope one day she will, but we can't force her to do anything, we can only help her see the beauty of it.

Tell the girls and Auntie I said hi, miss you guys!! I'll come visit soon, I promise.

He overdosed on heroin a week later, and I never got around to coming to visit. My mom's been clean since.

"BE good in school."
"don't WORRY, I will, POPs."

That's when we last talked before I went back to college for spring semester. He died four months later, on the same weekend I chose to go to my university's homecoming festival one state away from where he died. I still hate myself to this day for choosing the festival over going home.

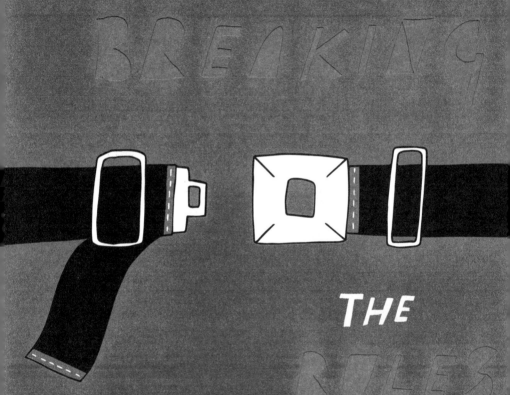

I'M BREAKING THE RULES

The last thing my best friend said to me over Snapchat on his way to spring break in Florida. He was lying down in the backseat, not wearing his seat belt. An hour later his family got into a crash and he was ejected from the car. He was pronounced brain dead the next day.

She was my best friend. We got into a huge fight and she ended it with this. I miss her sometimes, but then this text pops into my mind. I see her at practices twice a week and we don't speak, and I'm glad.

My grandmother's last words to my brother, my sister, and me. In the end she didn't always have a grasp on what she was saying, but I knew she meant this. All she ever wanted was to see us happy and successful. It's been close to five years, and I can't help thinking that I've let her down. Granny, I love you so much and I miss you every day. I hope you're proud of me. I really, really hope you're proud of me.

I'm sorry it was all too much.
I really hope you can forgive me.
Tell Dad I'm sorry but I couldn't
take it anymore. BE BRAVE.
I love you,
            little Sis.
                        x

The note I found cleaning out my sister's room a year after
she overdosed on pills. She died two weeks after my birthday
six years ago, and I'm still not sure if I've forgiven her.

I'M **not** HAPPY ANYMORE.

I **don't** OWE YOU AN EXPLANATION

goodbye.

We had been dating for over two
years, haven't heard from her since.

I JUST WANT TO BE ON MY OWN.

After three months of dating the guy I thought I was going to spend the rest of my life with, he sent me this. He'd starting distancing himself after I got really upset because someone I was very close to had passed away. He didn't understand grief, made me feel like I was stupid and pathetic, and wouldn't give me the closure I needed.

This was 18 months ago and I still think of him as my first real love and "what could have been" relationship.

The next day I saw him on a dating app; he clearly didn't want to be on his own.

you should
only get one
ticket to prom.

ADMIT ONE

I had asked the guy I was dating at the time to go to my high school prom. He went to a different school. His response was how he ended things with me. The next time I saw him he treated me like I was the scum of the earth. I ended up going to prom alone.

It's been eight years and I still don't know why he ended things. It still hurts.

Don't feel bad, I don't get along with anyone anyway.

He didn't even try for me, and I mentally exhausted myself for him.

COUNTRY MUSIC DOESN'T HELP the FEELING of MISSING YOU.

The first person who really showed me what love was. But we were at different places in our lives and it never would have worked.

have a good life. blocked.

I love you ALWAYS, SOULMATE.

This was the last message my ex-boyfriend sent me before I found out he had been dating someone else for months while he was telling me he loved me.

MAY, WE MEET AGAIN, I LOVE YOU, TO THE MOON AND BACK.

PS: PLEASE NEVER FORGET ME.

My best friend sent me this text one week ago after I asked someone to give her a letter I wrote. We haven't talked in one year since my girlfriend told me to stop talking to her. I miss her so much.

Please, don't ever text me back. I just want to forget you ever existed.

I Recycled th
LOVE LETTER
you sent me s
that the end of
OuR LOVE StOr
could be the
beginning of
someone else's.

I met a girl in my dreams last night who wasn't you, maybe she exists.

Anyways, if we ever cross paths again, try not to be a complete asshole.

Don't try to come back this time. 😊

The last thing my best friend said to me
after I blocked him on all social media.

YOU'RE MY BEST FRIEND IN THE WORLD

I JUST FEEL BETTER AROUND OTHER PEOPLE. I DON'T LIKE TALKING TO YOU.

She was my best friend. We did everything together. I still don't know what happened.

HEY,
angel face,

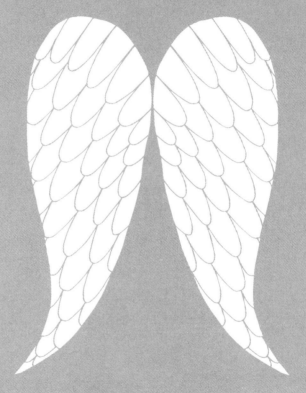

HOW ARE YOU?

The last message my mom sent me the night before she
killed herself. I ignored it to go to sleep, not knowing that
was going to be the last thing she would ever say to me.

TIME TO WAKE UP.

The last message my dad sent me before
he died. I didn't see it until a week later.

YOU ALWAYS HEAR
PEOPLE SAY YOU
KNOW WHEN YOU
MEET THE one and
It's true.
Something tells me
YOU'RE MY one.
I DIDN'T THINK I
COULD LOVE ANYTHING
as MUCH as I LOVE
YOU.

He never spoke to me again. A week later he had somebody new.

I know it's pathetic
but I just hope that
somewhere deep
down a little part
of you still misses
me more than you
love him.

I didn't have the heart to answer.

After months of tension and fighting, I put an end to an emotionally taxing and toxic friendship. I still believe I did the right thing for both of us, but there isn't a day that goes by where these words don't run through my head or I don't feel bad for how things ended.

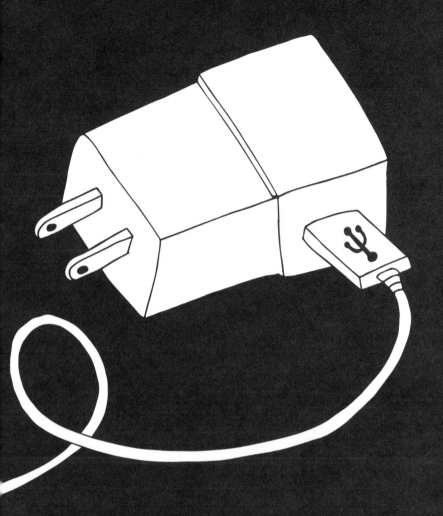

BRING ME MY PHONE CHARGER.

After I poured my heart out to my best
friend about how we were drifting apart.

YOU WERE THE ONLY PERSON WHO REALLY KNEW ME, KNEW THE THINGS I FELT AND WHO I REALLY WAS.

FIND A NEW SAVIOR, IT CAN'T BE ME ANYMORE.

She was convinced I'd always be there for her, even after she broke my heart. I had to finally say goodbye.

you're the best thing to
ever happen to me in life,
and the worst.
MOSTLY the WORST.

I CAN'T DO THIS ANYMORE.
NO MORE SAD SONGS.
NO MORE GOODBYES.

I USED TO LOOK FORWARD TO YOUR MESSAGES. I WANTED TO KNOW ABOUT YOUR DAY AND HOW YOU ARE. BUT NOW I JUST DON'T FEEL THE NEED ANYMORE.

He said as he broke my heart for what I hope is the last time.

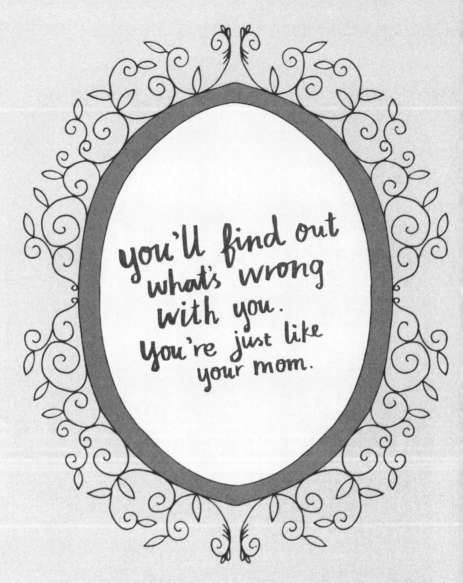

you'll find out what's wrong with you. You're just like your mom.

My dad after he kicked me out of his house, March 2015. I had left my mom's house in November 2014 when my dad convinced me to stay with him and his new wife. I have never felt more betrayed.

My mom's ex after years of telling me I was more like a daughter to him than his bio daughter. Also after finally standing up to him abusing me.

Sleepy-sounding, the voice of a 10-year-old girl who's pressed up against my side. She's small and delicate, like a little flower.

I was 12, and her older cousin and closest friend. We had stories about a princess who was a knight, whose prince was a dragon.

So I told her another story until she fell asleep, and tried my best not to panic (but simply to call out for her mother) when I felt her stop breathing.

Her name was Lucinde, and she had cancer, and she'll always be the princess who deserved the stories we created.

But I'm not your gorgeous girl anymore.

THE LAST MESSAGE RECEIVED SAVED MY LIFE

One of the most satisfying parts of creating The Last Message Received Tumblr is hearing about the closure and help it provides to both the people who submit their last messages and people who read the submissions of others. I've found that it's extremely helpful to people dealing with loss and grief—either because of the deaths of people close to them, or romantic or platonic breakups—to see that other people have survived going through something similar.

These messages from followers of The Last Message Received showcase how the community created by this Tumblr is helping people. It shows that by sharing some of the worst things you've gone through, you can help yourself and others.

WHENEVER I FEEL BAD ABOUT THE LAST MESSAGES I'VE RECEIVED FROM PEOPLE, I ALWAYS GO HERE AND READ WHAT PEOPLE HAVE SUBMITTED AND THEN I DON'T FEEL SO ALONE.

THE LAST MESSAGE ABOUT THE SISTER WHO COMMITTED SUICIDE REALLY HIT ME. I'VE BEEN FEELING LOST AND DEPRESSED LATELY, WHICH IS TAKING A TOLL. I'M GLAD I SAW THIS. I DON'T WANT TO LEAVE MY LITTLE BROTHER IN THAT MUCH PAIN. THANKS~!

GOING THROUGH THE WORST PERIOD OF MY LIFE SO FAR AND THIS PAGE IS LIKE A SAFE HAVEN, SOMEWHERE I DON'T FEEL ALONE EVEN IF IT'S FOR THREE MINUTES. THANK YOU.

THANK YOU, THANK YOU SO VERY MUCH FOR TAKING YOUR TIME TO HELP GIVE A VOICE TO THOSE WHO FEEL SILENCED, ALONE AND HURT. YOU HAVE NO IDEA HOW MANY LIVES YOU'VE SAVED THUS FAR BY GIVING PEOPLE LIKE ME, WHO FEEL LIKE THEIR ONLY/BEST OPTION IS TO END IT ALL, AN OUTLET

TO KNOW WE AREN'T ALONE IN OUR
TERRIBLE PAIN AND SUFFERING, AND
ALTHOUGH THE SITUATION MAY
NOT BE THE EXACT SAME, THE MESSAGE
BEHIND IT IS. THANK YOU FROM
THE BOTTOM OF MY HEART FOR
CARING, AND I HOPE YOU CONTINUE
DOING WONDERFUL THINGS. ♥

HEY! I JUST WANT TO SAY THANK YOU. I OCCASIONALLY HAVE THESE DEPRESSED PERIODS, AND THE LAST ONE WAS PRETTY BAD. READING THIS BLOG (AMONG OTHER THINGS) HAS HELPED ME VERY MUCH IN OVERCOMING IT. THANKS A BUNCH!!

OK, SO YOU PROBABLY DON'T REALLY CARE AND I'M SORRY TO BOTHER YOU, BUT YOUR BLOG LITERALLY SAVED MY LIFE. WHENEVER I'M FEELING SO DOWN THAT I WANT TO HURT MYSELF, I JUST COME HERE AND THINK THAT I DON'T WANT MY FAMILY TO HAVE TO PONDER OVER THE LAST THING I SAID TO THEM. LITERALLY, THIS IS WHY I'M HERE, BECAUSE EVERYONE SUBMITTING HAS FORCED ME TO REALIZE HOW SELFISH IT WOULD BE FOR ME TO DO THAT. THANKS FOR HELPING ME REALIZE THAT ALTHOUGH I FEEL ALONE NOW, PEOPLE WOULD REALLY MISS ME.

I AM JUST OUT OF A PSYCHIATRIC WARD AFTER HALF A YEAR OF SUICIDAL THOUGHTS AND SELF-HARM. THIS BLOG MAKES ME UNBELIEVABLY HAPPY, BECAUSE I NEVER SENT MY LAST MESSAGES. TALK TO THE PEOPLE YOU LOVE. THANK YOU!

I LOST MY DAD TO SUICIDE A MONTH AGO. WE HAD NO IDEA HE WAS SUFFERING AND HE LEFT NO SIGNS. ABOUT TWO WEEKS AGO I FOUND THIS BLOG AND SPENT HOURS AND HOURS SCROLLING THROUGH UNTIL 6AM READING ALL THE STORIES. IT HELPED ME SO MUCH TO REALIZE I'M NOT ALONE IN THIS, LIKE OTHER PEOPLE HAVE BEEN THROUGH SIMILAR THINGS AND SO CAN I. THANK YOU SO MUCH FOR MAKING THIS BLOG.

IS THERE A WAY I CAN LET SOME OF THESE SUBMITTERS KNOW THAT THEY ARE SO MUCH BETTER THAN THE WAYS THEIR "LOVED" ONES HAVE TREATED THEM? STOP PINING FOR THEM; ANYONE WHO DOESN'T WANT YOU IS NOT GOOD ENOUGH FOR YOU. ALSO, I DIDN'T REALIZE UNTIL READING SOME OF THESE THAT RELATIONSHIPS ARE SO FRAGILE. ANOTHER REASON TO TAKE CARE OF YOU AND BE TRUE TO YOURSELF. :)

SUBMIT YOUR LETTERS

Now that you've read this collection of messages, I hope they have inspired you to submit the last messages you have received. It is surprisingly cathartic, and you will be part of an ever-growing online community of support. Here's what you need to know to submit your message.

HOW DO I SUBMIT A MESSAGE?
You can use the submissions page: thelastmessagereceived.tumblr.com/submit. Or you can email it to lastmessagereceived@yahoo.com.

IS PROFANITY ALLOWED ON THE TUMBLR?
Yes.

DO YOU POST EVERY SUBMISSION?
I try my best to, but with thousands of submissions, it sometimes takes a while to post them. I am just one person!

IS IT ANONYMOUS?
Yes. I post all letters anonymously.

CAN I SUBMIT A VOICEMAIL?
Yes. You can submit a last voicemail received by emailing it to lastmessagereceived@yahoo.com. You can listen to the current voicemail submissions by going to soundcloud.com/thelastmessagereceived.

CAN I SUBMIT SOMETHING IN A LANGUAGE OTHER THAN ENGLISH?
Yes—submissions in your native language are completely fine.

I LOOK FORWARD TO HEARING FROM YOU.

RESOURCES

If you or someone you know needs help with depression or is having suicidal thoughts, there are numerous websites, organizations, and support networks out there. Below are just a few of those resources.

HOTLINES

BLOCH CANCER HOTLINE
1-800-433-0464 • *If you are newly diagnosed with cancer, the R. A. Bloch Cancer Foundation's helpline will answer your questions and match you with a survivor of your type of cancer for additional support.*

CHILDHELP NATIONAL CHILD ABUSE HOTLINE
1-800-4-A-CHILD (422-4453) • *Provides crisis intervention and professional counseling on child abuse.*

GLBT NATIONAL YOUTH TALKLINE
1-800-246-PRIDE (7743) • *A hotline where you can talk to peers about everything from relationship problems to bullying.*

NATIONAL ALLIANCE OF THE MENTALLY ILL
1-800-950-NAMI (6264) • *Trained volunteers provide information, referrals, and support to anyone with questions about mental illness.*

NATIONAL ASSOCIATION OF ANOREXIA NERVOSA & ASSOCIATED DISORDERS (ANAD)
1-630-577-1330 • *Advocates for the development of healthy attitudes, bodies, and behaviors who can assist in finding treatment.*

NATIONAL CANCER INSTITUTE CONTACT CENTER
1-800-4-CANCER (422-6237) • *Specialists are available to answer questions and provide information through NCI's LiveHelp online chat service.*

NATIONAL DOMESTIC VIOLENCE HOTLINE
1-800-799-SAFE (7233) • *Provides crisis intervention and referrals to local services and shelters for victims of abuse.*

NATIONAL SUICIDE PREVENTION LIFELINE
1-800-273-TALK (8255) • *A 24-hour service available to anyone in need of help.*

NATIONAL TEEN DATING ABUSE HELPLINE (LOVE IS RESPECT)
1-866-331-9474 • *A 24-hour resource for teens who have been abused.*

NATIONAL YOUTH CRISIS HOTLINE
1-800-448-4663 • *Provides short-term counseling for youth dealing with pregnancy, molestation, suicide, and child abuse.*

RAPE, ABUSE, AND INCEST NATIONAL NETWORK (RAINN)
1-800-656-HOPE (4673) • *Offers confidential, judgment-free support from a trained staff member, local resources that can assist with steps toward recovery, and sexual assault forensic exams.*

SUBSTANCE ABUSE AND MENTAL HEALTH SERVICES ADMINISTRATION (SAMHSA)
1-800-662-HELP (4357) • *Provides 24-hour services for individuals and family members facing mental health and substance use disorders.*

WEBSITES

AMERICAN CANCER SOCIETY
cancer.org • *Provides resources to help guide you through every step of the cancer experience.*

CANCERCARE
cancercare.org • *Provides free professional support services for caregivers and loved ones, as well as caregiving information and additional resources.*

THE DOUGY CENTER, THE NATIONAL CENTER FOR GRIEVING CHILDREN & FAMILIES
dougy.org • *Provides support in a safe place where children, teens, young adults, and their families can grieve and share their experiences.*

HOSPICE OF THE VALLEY, TEEN GRIEF SUPPORT
hov.org/teen-grief-support • *Provides help and counseling to teens who are working through grief.*

THE JASON FOUNDATION

jasonfoundation.com • *Provides information, education programs, and resources to help in the fight against the "silent epidemic" of youth suicide.*

LIVESTRONG

livestrong.org • *Provides emotional support and other resources for caregivers and patients.*

NARCOTICS ANONYMOUS

na.org • *Self-help group for drug addicts in treatment and recovery— open to substance abuse problems of all kinds.*

NATIONAL ALLIANCE ON MENTAL ILLNESS (NAMI)

nami.org • *A grassroots organization for people with mental illness and their families.*

NATIONAL EATING DISORDERS ASSOCIATION (NEDA)

nationaleatingdisorders.org • *An organization advocating for and supporting individuals and families affected by eating disorders.*

SMART RECOVERY (Self-Management and Recovery Training)

smartrecovery.org • *A program aimed to help people abstain from alcohol and drugs through a four-point program that encourages self-empowerment and positive thinking.*

SOCIETY FOR THE PREVENTION OF TEEN SUICIDE

sptsusa.org • *Encourages public awareness through the development and promotion of educational training programs.*

THE TREVOR PROJECT

thetrevorproject.org • *The number one organization for LGBTQ youth suicide prevention.*

> NOTE: *If you are worried about a suicidal friend or family member, visit the Warning Signs page on the Trevor Project website: thetrevorproject.org/pages/the-warning-signs*

YELLOW RIBBON SUICIDE PREVENTION PROGRAM

yellowribbon.org • *An organization that addresses youth/teen suicide through public awareness, education, and training to help communities build and strengthen suicide-prevention programs.*

BOOKS

Beyond the Blues: A Workbook to Help Teens Overcome Depression, by Lisa M. Schab, published by Instant Help, 2008.

Hello, Cruel World: 101 Alternatives to Suicide for Teens, Freaks, and Other Outlaws, by Kate Bornstein, published by Seven Stories Press, 2006.

If You Feel Too Much, by Jamie Tworkowski, published by TarcherPerigee, 2015.

It Gets Better, edited by Dan Savage and Terry Miller, published by Dutton, 2011.

My Anxious Mind: A Teen's Guide to Managing Anxiety and Panic, by Michael A. Tompkins and Katherine A. Martinez, published by Magination, 2010.

My Parent Has Cancer and It Really Sucks, by Maya Silver and Marc Silver, published by Sourcebooks Fire, 2013.

Queer: The Ultimate LGBT Guide for Teens, by Kathy Belge and Marke Bieschke, published by Zest Books, 2011.

Staying Strong: 365 Days a Year, by Demi Lovato, published by Feiwel and Friends, 2013.

This Star Won't Go Out: The Life & Words of Esther Grace Earl, by Esther Earl, published by Dutton Books for Young Readers, 2014.

We All Fall Down: Living with Addiction, by Nic Sheff, published by Little, Brown, 2011.

ACKNOWLEDGMENTS

Thank you first to everyone who's sent in their own last messages, or read the submissions others have sent in. You've all been integral in making this project possible, and in helping it change so many lives for the better. Thank you, from the bottom of my heart.

Second, I would like to thank some amazing people who have supported The Last Message Received, and me.

Thank you to Heather Flaherty, and the rest of the agents at The Bent Agency.

Thank you to Random House, especially Emily Easton, and everyone else involved in the publishing process.

Thank you to Rian, Misty, and Andy.

Thank you to Dad, Mom, Katie, Ashley, Courtney, Ethan, Rachel, Uncle Scott and Aunt Gina, Uncle Chris and Aunt Xiao Li, and the rest of my family.

ABOUT THE AUTHOR

Emily Trunko is an astonishing sixteen-year-old girl from the small town of Copley, Ohio. At age eleven, she started a book review called On Emily's Bookshelf, and at age fourteen she started the Clover Chain Project, dedicated to pairing up teens struggling with similar issues, which attracted local media attention. Emily created two Tumblr projects that became Internet sensations and books. Dear My Blank was inspired by her own personal notebook of letters that she wrote but never intended to send. And The Last Message Received grew out of her curiosity about life-changing letters, notes, and texts that people have received. Emily continues to be fascinated by the way people connect through the written word.

ABOUT THE ILLUSTRATOR

Zoë Ingram is a designer and illustrator from Adelaide, Australia, where her biggest inspiration is her two daughters. The sunshine, flora, and fauna of Australia also play a big part in her work. When she's not illustrating or designing patterns, Zoë, who studied printed textiles in Scotland, likes to stay in touch with her past by knitting, weaving, and painting.

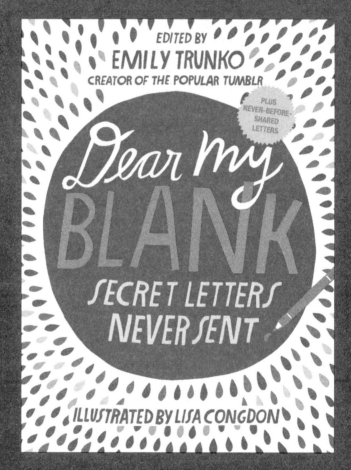